MW00425022

NEW
$14.00

A Fiddle Pulled
from the Throat
of a Sparrow

Noah Eli Gordon

New Issues Poetry & Prose

A Green Rose Book

New Issues Poetry & Prose
The College of Arts and Sciences
Western Michigan University
Kalamazoo, Michigan 49008

Copyright © 2007 by Noah Eli Gordon. All rights reserved.
Printed in the United States of America.

First Edition, 2007.

ISBN-10   1-930974-68-X (paperbound)
ISBN-13   978-1-930974-68-5 (paperbound)

Library of Congress Cataloging-in-Publication Data:
Gordon, Noah Eli
A Fiddle Pulled from the Throat of a Sparrow/Noah Eli Gordon
Library of Congress Control Number: 2006937310

Editor   Herbert Scott
Copy Editor   Elizabeth Marzoni
Managing Editor   Marianne Swierenga
Designer   Alynn Ramoie
Art Director   Tricia Hennessy
Production Manager   Paul Sizer
                              The Design Center, School of Art
                              College of Fine Arts
                              Western Michigan University

A Fiddle Pulled from the Throat of a Sparrow

Noah Eli Gordon

New Issues

 WESTERN MICHIGAN UNIVERSITY

Also by Noah Eli Gordon

Books:

The Frequencies
The Area of Sound Called the Subtone
Inbox
Novel Pictorial Noise
Figures for a Darkroom Voice
    (with Joshua Marie Wilkinson)

Chapbooks and Limited Edition Pamphlets:

The Fire & The Blue
    (with Nick Moudry)
The Laughing Alphabet
Untitled (Whalebone) Essays
    (with Eric Baus, Nick Moudry, and Travis Nichols)
Notes Toward the Spectacle
Jaywalking the Is
What Ever Belongs in the Circle
how human nouns
Twenty Ruptured Paragraphs from a Perfectly Functional Book
That We Come to a Consensus
    (with Sara Veglahn)
A New Hymn to the Old Night
    (split release with Michael Friedman's "A Line Drive to Left")
Flag

for Joshua Marie Wilkinson

Contents

A Dictionary of Music

A fiddle pulled from the throat of a sparrow   7
Phrasing and form   8
By the sound of rose leaves clapped against the palms 9
A tuning fork turns all this noise to glass   10
A falling in autumn   11
An exact comprehension of the composer's intent   12

The Right of Return

The book of journeys   17
The book of forgetting   18
The book of rebuilding   19
The book of definitions   20
The book of signs   21
The book of trades   22
The book of hunger   23
Postscript: the book of Cain   24

How Human Nouns

They said the smallest wooden horse was dead
          in your costume   29
A point of view apart from a personal embrace   30
To map the wearing away of things   31
The forest burns into later time   32
Nothing under the stones but the story of lifting   33
A due measure of duration   34
One event collapses into another's unsaid   35
It was raining near dusk & I was still reading   36
Simple as a wall painted blue   37
Figuration in conflict with an afternoon   38
An approximation of the actual letter   39
If there is always a room's reversal of events   40

Untragic Hero of Epic Theater 43

Four Allusive Fields 51

Book of Names 59

A New Hymn to the Old Night 73

A Little Book of Prayers

    Dove song 87
    A black mirror for the capital 88
    Urge to call 89

A Dictionary of Music

A fiddle pulled from the throat of a sparrow

little piece of silence

astray in the circumstantial music of a crowd

part myth, part massacre

have you put away your toy internment

turned to the first movement

where the house was empty

& the dead hair of the harpist spread on the lawn

its arrayed core drawing a grace note

from the muttering of those exhausted by wild dance

showing an oar for a lyre

a turtle shell a tear

cleaving a bird call on the kettle drum

to unsettle a dust of harmonics

expelling an itinerant elsewhere

an epistolary scratching-post

a winged thing for the gypsy's chime

the timbrel's return to nowhere

Phrasing and form

the landlord calls this part an opera

        sharp geometry, an X punctuating the calendar

the dusted shaft of dying light

        dust on the surface, on everything

everything suspect, already ash

        the terrible skull under such a pretty face

that diner used to be a train car

        that train an inkling of expansion

everything pretty transitive, aleatoric

        a row of candles in a sun-filled room

finality uncomfortably funny

        the landscape, a cathartic duet

acquiescent to the order of the day

        or plain unaware: stupid rock, stupid air

By the sound of rose leaves clapped against the palms

A ring of clarinets could draw out
the wolves, mimic a boat

growing smaller. A syllable
in which an ocean rests.

Reeds, buckling with wind.
They've set ballerinas dancing

on deck. A glass anchor,
molded in the shape of a ruined mouth:

These are stairways, starways—
ways of ascension, it might say

or try to say. Its voice erased
by drought, by doubt.

Bent notes keep the wolves at bay,
fallen petals mistaken for a fuse.

A wheel rubbed in resin
drawn across catgut strings

for fodder from the flaired bells
to lose the conductor where melody begins.

A tuning fork turns all this noise to glass

bangles knock against
    the broken neck of a cello

& they return
    to a dying theme, detailing air—

a dance as old
    as the circle, antique

poison of a dead wasp,
    its wound potential

miming the music
of one digging a ditch,

the rough sketch
    of an abbreviated calm,

a further conjugation of focus
or just something to fill the afternoon—

all this work on balance,
an anodyne for falling in

A falling in autumn

felt as a mistake

in translation:

leave for *leaf*

so the tree is an exit

a door into weather

An exact comprehension of the composer's intent

Cloudless sky, a tendril root, a chord begun
    as unfolding duration & one's lost words,
a red lexicon, an empty definition

gathering its discourse—the flow from content
    to perception: language is a translation of grace.
Say the body, say the heart, a composition in blue,

the passing energy, cell, motion, inevitability;
    an impact until meaning wears through
the mind's opulence, its spindle—a white thread.

Tethered to conviction, one says moon, one, emotion
    —the recurrence of night: a door will open,
shifting from anonymity to intellection—a translation

of sight with speech, awoken not by voice
    but what precedes it: the worldliness, wordless;
a measure of sound or movement to song.

The Right of Return

The book of journeys

The body became a voyage,
              became the thought of god
as the beginning of a circle,
          thought that was the desert,
         that was found there in thirst

With clocks on the walls,
             the arrangements wrong,
each star seemed off kilter,
        so their maps receded,
        sent footprints into sand

Somewhere the boat disappeared
              & fires were set in a village;
some came down for the dance;
        some hid in the haylofts,
        at the river, at the mouth—the teeth,
its source: a thimbleful of silt in the eyes

One said the shore meant a corroding,
              roots beginning to show an edge
through soil, how a hole
        can cleave into what was whole
        like sand, glass; the embers gone black,
unlike a mirror or what a window knows,

but the oars, the oars were carved out of bone

The book of forgetting

Sun-bleached into memory,
ribbon scars—
    a notch for the bloodletting table,
& each knot, loosened:
    ropes gone slack

Payment in a pound of flesh;
how a breath links its fingers
    —the canary quieted,
called: history gone down
    —buried to the hilt

Extraction without a drop,
hooks & curves for tearing,
    learned retrieval,
an empty suitcase or pile of shoes,
    soot-nails & tongue-salt

The veins, a sea;
open-valved & splayed,
    two wings of red velvet
called a cool heart,
    though culled,
both blood-deep & drifting

The book of rebuilding

They stood at the base of the ladder afraid of its scorching rungs

The tablet they found read:

   a month of fruit harvest
a month of sowing
   one of after-grass

Abeyance as the space for a single coin

Knew they weren't always wanderers,
paid for the ferry with cracks in the walls,
with light to make out each marking:

a month of flax harvest,
   of barley harvest
(a blue-inked incision line)
   a month of everything else . . .

to ash, to an alphabet of palm-worn tools, a fistful of permanence

Call this the point of view:
   the border of threads,
the locks, a language of gears,
   void, unpunctuated—the round peg . . .
& deeper . . .

learned a counter motion,
   an unearthing, against the theory
of stones—how they stack well

The book of definitions

The vestigial mark was the word

shadow in the preface

though they circled around the flame,

thought of this night

took form first as bone,

first a cliff overlooking the sea

called "longing for arrival"

When the youngest asked

why this hand was different from others,

another drew in his fingers & said

"This hand is called a fist."

Not to take note but to transcribe

Bells were rung & special knots devised

The book of signs

Icons were no longer icons
& their eye-sacks unlaced
In the field, testing the full range of motion
All wicks removed, each stump sanded down
Stripped of rank & arms at their sides,
counted each ring, regardless
their equivalent for the word winter

Collected shoes called acceptable losses,
so without hitting the bottom
the next sign read: lasso, lash, lesson
Still, one went on playing her violin
Slits cut in hems & bricks left unstacked
Icons were icons & the book remained open

The book of trades

Splitting leather,
recalled a place for anyone good

with a needle, with a finger . . .
all matter in flux

A coin recast into a bullet,
distraction in a direct source of light

Some luck not to inherit
the features, curls thick as iron

A train like a halo took a pound
of flesh without a drop of blood

Written on loose clothing,
the book worn in the wind

The book of hunger

the sound of smoke

was that of expansion

but the breaking of bread

like a dusk-shadow

became a name

losing itself in echo

until there was no sound

but the snapping

etched into each rib

which repeats:

dust . . .   dust . . .   dust . . .

Postscript: the book of Cain

He took the train to an empty field which was not empty when an older train arrived years ago. The book explained: *to verbify a word is to put it into action, to incinerate its core meaning, allowing it to drift.* Once, he tried to swallow a stone: "No bigger than a fingernail," he said, "no bigger." The book continued as did the weeds. The rails. The cities. The songs. The songs. The singing.   ing.   .

How Human Nouns

We have nothing in common except the illusion of being together.

—Raoul Vaneigem, *The Revolution of Everyday Life*

All this has so much to do with grammar and with poetry and with prose.

—Gertrude Stein, *Lectures in America*

They said the smallest wooden horse was dead in your costume

gone unnoticed the inevitable protagonists accrue

fragile centipede working rot into unreliable endnotes

a storm, cicadas, ribbons of smoke above the river

somewhere else a war

light falls as usual

& the hour fails to be episodic

in the most expensive suit I've ever worn

A point of view apart from a personal embrace

watching the unfolding of an envelope

a red thread from a felt purse

landscape pulled in increments

or another anchor to architecture love

to the voice-over of someone older

if this desire for narrative outweighed

our unwillingness to concede an end

To map the wearing away of things

what endows an anecdote with so much tinder

a particular tree in how light fell

how human nouns what the nucleus of commerce won't replicate

the world in a real enough window

money made of money a bare ankle

pacing from the vault to the podium

to fasten the world a believable cape

The forest burns into later time

all that I saw from the balcony

an evening's warranted fiction yoked

little lamb that gathers & gathers against a half-eaten idea

I'm writing from the weather

inside a dictionary of difficult words

details solidify with each retelling

but someone coughs & the theater caves in

Nothing under the stones but the story of lifting

in one scene we stood on a bridge

watching boats catch in their sails late wedges of light

there was grace, ease, a hero's mask assembled

from an hour's background music

our inclination to trail a supposed mother toward the concrete

a crow calls out its lineage

a surrogate thorn   an imperfect Xerox

A due measure of duration

already dusk bringing a different feeling

to the scuttle of leaves, billboards outlining the city

outliving directives in a little book of prayers

a cue to place the pencil down & wait

for the refrain to repeat itself

somehow we sustain history

one hand making a fist, two a steeple

One event collapses into another's unsaid

an evening worn on the locality of thinking

imagined as a tactile day-moon

unanchored as I am

by letters, books, creased sheet music

cicadas' shells lodged between lengths of sawed lumber

the public they, gloved in expectancy

O sweet Rashomon, it is thick & manageable & perpetual

It was raining near dusk & I was still reading

from a window painted shut to a woodcut

of the player's fingers nailed to a flute

beautiful as laugh tracks alone with our wallets

I'd call you uncomfortable in dress shoes

while the night comes undone waiting

still there is lightning & inevitable rot

the pronoun's shadow—its dark lake

Simple as a wall painted blue

scaled from sovereignty to ethos

the logic of a button worn from overuse

I'd change my shirt to say "story of the day"

like a coin that previously fit the slot no longer deserving

another city's disorder or the bird's moronic circles

evolving a gentle etymology of sky

memory comes to sister the missing handles

Figuration in conflict with an afternoon

whose you is a whisper all verb

whose you a child's hair in flames

whose you is replacing a curtain

whose you is thickening the mortar

whose you imprinting a beating heart

whose you aged a flower

who found it dried in the center of a book

An approximation of the actual letter

I died in a book

& couldn't touch the ink around me

it was autumn

I died in a book asking

the word for leaf for leave

I died in a book on the eve of music

in the distance, another distance

If there is always a room's reversal of events

a painted-over presence from ear to understanding

what won't wash in the agreed-upon outcome

of a stand-in for our refusal of silhouettes

spilling momentous into scenery

a still-life not so gone to greener pastures

that I can't forgive myself an afternoon

unlocked unbroken untangled unaired

Untragic Hero of Epic Theater

Did blanched afternoon unfastening its oiled feathers
leave a trace of warmth in scurrying hooves
or was it a display window where a bee stumbling
between bits of jewelry stopped you from dabbling
in shiny pocket change

Glorious indifference! Hapless providence!
The subtlest lion makes the loudest flower & these
knotted gaudy defeats invert another gray century
photographing a statue's features rubbed clean

But what could we do with colorized mandolins
Whispers of a secret war sound identical in electric light
& something variegated is always happening in fashions
Continue to the next page & ignore what's behind the curtain
The imperative's wax center & a magnifying glass held to the sun

My machinery has a terrible horse
There are twisted fibers
ruts dug in the road made for mules
bricks rearranged to create a "sense of place"
& this cloud resembling a Roman column
It's enough to be on stage with a rifle
with dimmed lights relaxing the audience
Brushstrokes of smoke drift in sepia
& a man in uniform waves past
the idea of war to grace a wilderness
where columns of grass becoming a yard
became the foundation for a claim
to portray what erects a castle
around the already crumbling stage

So architecture's never idle
eats itself like a circle completely filled
or history taught as a series of paintings
in which all heads are removed

Give me dust on a white piano!
Give a few oranges the dirt!
Sirens blare through an open market
& the telephone's interrupting everything

What's the difference hedges toward a structure
I don't want the locution of some scuffed surface
just your lips moving like birds
where birds are not the story
second to its telling but the inky shape
of astonishment arresting our attention

How simply an antecedent of the last act
develops indifference itself, devolves the view
wedged gently (if there is such a thing)
through fleshy floorboards & sleeps on a small chair
on a dais with a flower folded in half

Here is your ladder & the word dilatancy
notice how as you go up the rungs disappear
how curtains rose to an indiscretion, anxious looks
& the look of anxiety, though act two saw actors
enter through the audience & rain coiled the day
indoors, carried bundles, was backstage
Come in, I'm sure the earth's still spinning
Hello helicopter! Hello trees!
The chandelier is something

Four Allusive Fields

Who is Cy Twombly? What is it he does?
And what are we to call what he does?

—Roland Barthes

Cy listens absently to absent Homer
& his refusal become a dead thing full of music
Smash it on a cyclotron. Drag it across a dozen centuries
Drips are old. Smudges are old. Talking a museum
out of its eternal monologue, it's not embarrassing
to leak in waves & cones. Nudes fall from newspapers
as you fell from an oily twilight, from a painting
of the word twilight, arranged without letters, inkless
like a fire that consumes all before it, or better, inkless
as the phrase: "like a fire that consumes all before it"
Who wouldn't be mayor of a worked-over surface
returning clutter for a broom, ever-after for Cliffs Notes
Work smudging talk; talk smudging work
Obedience is an awful word I think to get lost in

Cy listens absently to absent Homer
explaining himself away. Boring as a canvas
to a waterfall, as a splotch of red to equations
lifting a helicopter, injured by a display of attentiveness
can you believe this humming anonymous light
The light is anonymity. Break it against
an electron, smear it with a magpie's
greenish-black tail feather, cast it on a sheet
of orange vellum pasted inside a brown leather book
A cricket's ankle is not fragile to the cricket
Dab it there. It has nothing to do with the sun
The sun is a system free from authority
& you sweet shy Achilles have already worn
through your shoes & the pedestal beneath

Cy listens absently to absent Homer
taking notes that amount to nothing, & nothing
erases as well as a name. Can one draw a careless world
out of its engorged abdomen? Ask that moth
eating through a painted magpie what grinding
against a shard of twilight gave it. Flowers
chalked over aluminum & the elegance
of taped-on wings. Ladders reaching the roof
behind rain clouds brushed on to cover a mistake
Who wouldn't mistake the surface for vapid paint
a cloud for a sarcophagus a bed for a life your white shirt
for mine, blue for blue. Depending on the vantage point
proves you hang from it in pieces, & though we hadn't
arrived on the same boat, we're surely on the same boat now

Cy listens absently to absent Homer
regards a useless allegory spreading its human shape
across inaudible dirt. Sparse, porous, scattered
any moment's fringe epicenter is irredeemably stalling
& you move away like a building or a horse
The useless allegory adheres to logic, the first principle
of representation: if you walk to the bridge & refuse the view
clouds of blue steam still billow from a grate
below a green dumpster. Ask grime on a limbless statue
surrounded by tulips in May & hope for an end to winter
who doesn't age absently ignoring unhinged flesh
Nakedness is a carriage & I'm in love with impossibility
for its dynamic body. A shard of twilight smashed
on the cyclotron. If you can see the fibers don't say so

Book of Names

Why Bernadette? & why David?
Why Rebecca? Why Mark?
Why the book of names? Why say yes and no?
Why a syllable & its buoyancy?

Everything
Bernadette

is a spectacle

& soon the trees
outside

are still
the trees outside

Withdraw to a room
in which snow falls

No David—
          no I won't

since
sitting there

          blissful

your doubts
erase it

Blinds bring a quarter-inch world
itinerant architecture

The most complex organ
wants only to be

touched, teased a bit

& birds would hate
the singularity
of their idiot noise

if it were us
who'd built them

Allow the little ghosts
Duration's their say

Allowing the little ghosts
their everything

There—
          everything
& anti-everything

Yesterday
I named

a dead bird
Rebecca

Yes, I've said
or thought to say

Yes, I've said
nothing & then not

nothing, nothing
of our dusty thoughts

their harmonious
dismantling

of a girl
breathing

into an
umbrella

of a boy
covered in mud

cross-legged
under an ash tree

Nothing of ash
in the shape
of his tongue

or the tongue
of a small elephant
crossing the deserts

of Libya & Liberia
of the Gold Coast
& the Silver Coast

the tarnished coasts
of Toledo, Detroit
Little Tennesee

& the ghostlike
stone face of Hölderlin
disappearing

into an iron sky
into an element
of discourse

arranging a house
into a house whose
arrangement is elemental

This bed might be a lung
This desk a lifeboat

Dear Mark, tell Michael
I have lived many years

without windows
watching daily

from the second floor
waves devouring the shore

Were a defused heart
wintering the clock

time kept
by counting birds

I'd call flight
a half-belief in air

a venomous lack
when the ticking is less so

Why George? Why Cy?
Why do nudes fall from newspapers?
Why a fire that consumes all before it?
Why yes? & why no?
Why the world's most believable cape?

A New Hymn to the Old Night

Fernab liegt die Welt

—Novalis, *Hymnen an die Nacht*

afar lies the world

or down over there, far, lies the world

or the world lies to us Novalis

dead as waking day in joyous light

or just covered in glitter

part cliché, part cage

part musky smell of dust burning off the radiator

another November, another animal moving across the earth

another breeze & someone to call it gentle

any stranger, any shapely mouth, any sound dissolving to noise

noise & its fringe theater sustaining an open call

gull against those clouds, pebble lodged in a sneaker's tread

who isn't a boy in party dress in presence's wide drama

another mark on paper & someone to learn the names

another character gone to the season's closer

snow in the garden on the television facing the window near the taxi stand

snow on the staircase in the house on the ruined street where the novel ends

blue black night, blue-black distant constellations

& someone to call the camp fires happiness

to cull vapid contingencies from vapid rainfall

annulling a vapid image in place of itself

replacing vacancy in one's unwokenness

you try explaining a computer to the long dead

forget almond trees, grapes & poppies

what he wouldn't believe is the inescapable music here

the night filling with beloved firetrucks

cover your ears to cover the passing sirens

praise the passing sirens

afar lies the world

or down over there, far, lies the world

or the world lies against the empirical

against two notes escaping the drama of a dented harmonic

& the music that begins when they find a third

when the balance of an egret

pasted above day's unadorned particulars

stirs a folk song in this thimbleful of serum

begin with a boy on a park bench practicing adult exuberance

& end as the ear disallows before & after to enter an heirloom of song

an invention of the world wearing an allusion suspect

the earth a synonym for self, for you are here & otherwise

afar lies the world

or down over there, far, lies the world

or the world and its lies, too ashamed

to repeat the word endure to a doctrine

ending halfway across the Bay Bridge in a pair of old Reeboks

Liberty's detached head dying a beacon to virtue

leaving the taint and flaw of a story

the worth of a stone, canned sardines, and kerosene

can you conjugate autonomy without donning a coarse cloak

a widow's headdress, other ways to walk a life

hailing all ancillary images, how proudly they falter

why is every digression an illustrated history

why is every example a commonwealth in alternate translation

how can you separate bird from flock

the dock where a muddy tugboat's dislodged

from the evening the captain doesn't come home

the night from the sound of passing sirens

praise the passing sirens

praise clouds in the shape of a nightlight

praise meticulousness

praise the trail of the centipede

& the impulsive curve of a halo in impasto on paper

& pursue the legibility of all signs

endless morning's eroded surface & the surface of ordinary sense

praise the redundancy of self-ascribed visionaries pursuing burning dictionaries

is it better to be careful or to care only for fullness

the dog's head drops in shame, cocks in question

praise human complication's damaged form

receding from fight or flight to leaky cathedral

perfect as a linoleum print of lifelike grass

& the wind ribboning an afternoon straight out of Seurat

yield to passing traffic then praise the passing traffic

they look so small down there

soaked in linseed oil, semi-translucent

through the smeared window of a newspaper box

across headlines large as water towers

painted in tandem with a clear day

the quiet house & calm world, too, are deserving of praise

praise the roof against which breaks urbanity & pursue the joyous leak

praise the house, the keeper of the house & those for whom the house is kept

praise Mexico, go to Mexico, be continuously afraid of nothing

find Pancho Villa's Dodge, plastered with bullet holes

proud as supreme realism condensed in the face of a blue flower what's luminous about a clock, what's a spiky detail

which is worse, the balance beam or the laser beam

dreams don't bring back the dead

they affix microphones to iconography

praising the tissue of sleep, pleated as Sophie's rotting hair

praise wickedness in clocks, sun & all variants on rooftops

the most beautiful insects can only sting once

praise the beautiful insects

the most beautiful insects can only sting once

praise the exhaustion of the most beautiful insects

A Little Book of Prayers

Dove song

A dove makes a sentence in the window
unendurably the lack of dove

This plausible form thinks itself a garden
predicate to the shape of dove ideas

Now the air is thick, internal
A dove makes a sentence in the window

& a dove-made, noun-less conjecture
makes of the thinker a vacant dove sound

This plausible form thinks itself a garden
unpunctuated by reckless duration

reiterated from margin to margin, where
a dove makes a sentence in the window

unrestrained, a concerted dimmer silence
The weight of dove & the waiting dove

A black mirror for the capital

Decision can still clock hands
The moment, a voluminous straightjacket

Green gears of a gray earth
warped in the flick of a wrist

Rubble, a suffix for the burning city
a coat stitched from worn strikepads

You've seen the girl, naked & screaming
arms splayed as though she could take flight

from the road—from this heat
how it raises a map of welts:

the blueprint for a massive ark

Urge to call

Cohere who can say
—Myung Mi Kim

begin with the phrase: it's light outside

with a window, the reshaping of water

to map the shoreline between finger & figure

to say there is so much loss in the current

anchor-ripped coral or coral-ripped hull

adjacent, resolute, an idea preceding vocabulary

the inclination of a knee to bend or body to decay

one would question sleep as one would step

an image, angled—inverted in a spoon

the subject, suspect of syntax

one tests the wind with a finger as a ship settles

between shoreline & the lines on a map

the terms, twinned to coax out meaning

the leakage of water through slats of wood

one must begin with the current, the word cohere

a child who says: the window shows it's time to get up

Acknowledgements

The poems in this book, composed between 1999 & 2005, originally appeared, often in radically different versions and under different titles, in the following journals: *580 Split*, *88*, *Alice Blue Review*, *Bling Bling*, *Colorado Review*, *Hambone*, *LIT*, *Parnassus*, *Phoebe*, *Private* (Italy), *Shiny Magazine*, *Upstairs at Duroc* (France), *Ur-Vox*, *Versal* (The Netherlands), *Volt*, *WEB CONJUNCTIONS*, *Weird Deer*, and *Word For / Word*.

Earlier drafts of several of these poems were published as the chapbook *notes toward the spectacle* (Duration Press). "A falling in autumn" appeared along with a reproduction of Peter Gregorio's painting *Temporal Archway* in the Cloud-type postcard series. "How Human Nouns" appeared as a pamphlet in the PO25¢EM series. An earlier version of "A New Hymn to the Old Night" appeared with Michael Friedman's "A Line Drive to Left" as a chapbook published in conjunction with the Left Hand Reading Series in Boulder, Colorado. "Untragic Hero of Epic Theater" and "Four Allusive Fields" appeared in a pamphlet published in conjunction with the Hot Whiskey Reading Series.

Robert Creeley selected an earlier version of "A Dictionary of Music" for the Greg Grummer Prize from *Phoebe*. Carolyn Forché selected an earlier version of "A black mirror for the capital" for the Randall Jarrell Prize from the North Carolina Writer's Network. David Shapiro selected portions of this manuscript for the Glosband Fellowship in Poetry from the MFA Program for Poets & Writers at The University of Massachusetts at Amherst. Thanks to Jim Tate for helping me see that the title for this book was under my nose all the while.

photo by Ravi Durbeej

Noah Eli Gordon's books include *Novel Pictorial Noise* (selected by John Ashbery for the 2006 National Poetry Series), *Inbox* (BlazeVOX, 2006), *The Area of Sound Called the Subtone* (Ahsahta Press, 2004; selected by Claudia Rankine for the Sawtooth Prize), and *The Frequencies* (Tougher Disguises, 2003). Ugly Duckling Presse recently published *That We Come To A Consensus*, a chapbook written in collaboration with Sara Veglahn. His reviews and essays have appeared in dozens of journals, including *Boston Review*, *The Poker*, *26*, *Jacket*, and *The Poetry Project Newsletter*. He writes a chapbook review column for *Rain Taxi*, and teaches at the University of Colorado at Denver.

New Issues Poetry

Vito Aiuto, *Self-Portrait as Jerry Quarry*
James Armstrong, *Monument in a Summer Hat*
Claire Bateman, *Clumsy; Leap*
Kevin Boyle, *A Home for Wayward Girls*
Jason Bredle, *Standing in Line for the Beast*
Michael Burkard, *Pennsylvania Collection Agency*
Christopher Bursk, *Ovid at Fifteen*
Anthony Butts, *Fifth Season; Little Low Heaven*
Kevin Cantwell, *Something Black in the Green Part of Your Eye*
Gladys Cardiff, *A Bare Unpainted Table*
Kevin Clark, *In the Evening of No Warning*
Cynie Cory, *American Girl*
Peter Covino, *Cut Off the Ears of Winter*
James D'Agostino, *Nude with Anything*
Jim Daniels, *Night with Drive-By Shooting Stars*
Joseph Featherstone, *Brace's Cove*
Lisa Fishman, *The Deep Heart's Core Is a Suitcase*
Noah Eli Gordon, *A Fiddle Pulled from the Throat of a Sparrow*
Robert Grunst, *The Smallest Bird in North America*
Paul Guest, *The Resurrection of the Body and the Ruin of the World*
Robert Haight, *Emergences and Spinner Falls*
Mark Halperin, *Time as Distance*
Myronn Hardy, *Approaching the Center*
Brian Henry, *Graft*
Edward Haworth Hoeppner, *Rain Through High Windows*
Cynthia Hogue, *Flux*
Joan Houlihan, *The Mending Worm*
Christine Hume, *Alaskaphrenia*
Josie Kearns, *New Numbers*
David Keplinger, *The Clearing; The Prayers of Others*
Maurice Kilwein Guevara, *Autobiography of So-and-So: Poems in Prose*
Ruth Ellen Kocher, *When the Moon Knows You're Wandering;
    One Girl Babylon*
Gerry LaFemina, *The Window Facing Winter*
Steve Langan, *Freezing*
Lance Larsen, *Erasable Walls*
David Dodd Lee, *Abrupt Rural; Downsides of Fish Culture*
M.L. Liebler, *The Moon a Box*
Alexander Long, *Vigil*
Deanne Lundin, *The Ginseng Hunter's Notebook*
Carrie McGath, *Small Murders*
Barbara Maloutas, *In a Combination of Practices*
Joy Manesiotis, *They Sing to Her Bones*
Sarah Mangold, *Household Mechanics*

Gail Martin, *The Hourglass Heart*
David Marlatt, *A Hog Slaughtering Woman*
Louise Mathias, *Lark Apprentice*
Gretchen Mattox, *Buddha Box; Goodnight Architecture*
Paula McLain, *Less of Her; Stumble, Gorgeous*
Lydia Melvin, *South of Here*
Sarah Messer, *Bandit Letters*
Wayne Miller, *Only the Senses Sleep*
Malena Mörling, *Ocean Avenue*
Julie Moulds, *The Woman with a Cubed Head*
Marsha de la O, *Black Hope*
C. Mikal Oness, *Water Becomes Bone*
Bradley Paul, *The Obvious*
Jennifer Perrine, *The Body Is No Machine*
Katie Peterson, *This One Tree*
Elizabeth Powell, *The Republic of Self*
Margaret Rabb, *Granite Dives*
Rebecca Reynolds, *Daughter of the Hangnail; The Bovine Two-Step*
Martha Rhodes, *Perfect Disappearance*
Beth Roberts, *Brief Moral History in Blue*
John Rybicki, *Traveling at High Speeds* (expanded second edition)
Mary Ann Samyn, *Inside the Yellow Dress; Purr*
Ever Saskya, *The Porch is a Journey Different from the House*
Mark Scott, *Tactile Values*
Hugh Seidman, *Somebody Stand Up and Sing*
Martha Serpas, *Côte Blanche*
Diane Seuss-Brakeman, *It Blows You Hollow*
Elaine Sexton, *Sleuth*
Marc Sheehan, *Greatest Hits*
Heidi Lynn Staples, *Guess Can Gallop*
Phillip Sterling, *Mutual Shores*
Angela Sorby, *Distance Learning*
Matthew Thorburn, *Subject to Change*
Russell Thorburn, *Approximate Desire*
Rodney Torreson, *A Breathable Light*
Robert VanderMolen, *Breath*
Martin Walls, *Small Human Detail in Care of National Trust*
Patricia Jabbeh Wesley, *Before the Palm Could Bloom: Poems of Africa*